Wendy Susan Deaton, MA, MFT
Michael Hertica, MS, MFT

Growing Free
A Manual for Survivors of Domestic Violence

Pre-publication
REVIEWS,
COMMENTARIES,
EVALUATIONS . . .

"**A**s a nurse educator, I will make *Growing Free* required reading for nursing students at all levels of education. Nurses are in a unique position to intervene in domestic violence. Simply giving this manual to a client who seems to be suffering in a relationship would be a powerful thing to do. Reading this text may also give some students insight into their own experiences and encourage them to apply the authors' suggestions to circumstances in which they can identify coercion, verbal abuse, or humiliation whether at work, in training, or in their family."

Beatrice Crofts Yorker, RN, JD
Professor of Nursing,
Georgia State University,
Decatur

"**I**n *Growing Free*, the authors have captured the essence of what survivors really need—recognition of their struggle, information on the big picture, and clear options about what they can do now. The simple outline of safety plans under a variety of conditions makes a complex subject manageable. Most important, the authors address the 'how to' of rebuilding one's life.

This is a necessary book for anyone who is scared and starting to think about what it would take to 'grow free.' Friends and relatives of a person in a domestic violence situation can use this very helpful book as a guide. I recommend it highly."

Colleen Friend, LCSW
Field Work Consultant,
UCLA Department
of Social Welfare,
School of Public Policy
& Social Research

Growing Free
A Manual for Survivors
of Domestic Violence

Growing Free
A Manual for Survivors
of Domestic Violence

Wendy Susan Deaton, MA, MFT
Michael Hertica, MS, MFT

HMTP

The Haworth Maltreatment and Trauma Press®
An Imprint of The Haworth Press, Inc.
New York • London • Oxford

Published by

The Haworth Maltreatment and Trauma Press®, an imprint of The Haworth Press, Inc., 10 Alice Street, Binghamton, NY 13904-1580.

Cover design by Jennifer M. Gaska.

Library of Congress Cataloging-in-Publication Data

Deaton, Wendy.
    Growing free : a manual for survivors of domestic violence / Wendy Susan Deaton, Michael Hertica.
       p. cm.
    Includes bibliographical references and index.
    ISBN 0-7890-1280-4 (soft : alk. paper)
    1. Family violence—Psychological aspects. 2. Victims of family violence—Psychology.
    I. Title: Manual for survivors of domestic violence. II. Hertica, Michael. III. Title.

HV6626 .D43 2001
362.82'924—dc21
                                         00-047212

To Summer and Heather,
May your futures be free of violence
and full of serenity.
Love, Nana

To 1736,
Nicole and Curtis,
Thanks, Mike

ABOUT THE AUTHORS

Wendy Susan Deaton, MA, MFT, has been a licensed marriage and family therapist in private practice since 1982. She has worked with the entire range of victimization and abuse, including treatment for individuals and training for law enforcement, district attorneys, social workers, rape crisis and shelter personnel, and medical and mental health providers. Wendy's professional publications include two editions of the *Child Sexual Abuse Dispute Annotated Bibliography* and the *Growth and Recovery Workbooks,* a series of therapeutic journals for children. The *Growth and Recovery* series includes workbooks devoted to living with domestic violence, sexual abuse, and other types of trauma witnessed and experienced by children. Her professional articles have appeared in the *CAPSAC Consultant,* the *ASPAC Advisor,* and the *Nurse Practitioner Forum.* She has been on the Board of Directors of the California Professional Society on the Abuse of Children (CAPSAC) since 1993.

Lieutenant Michael Hertica, MS, MFT, is retired from the Torrance Police Department where he worked from 1969-1999. Lt. Hertica is an instructor in the investigation of child abuse and domestic violence cases. He has trained at conferences and for agencies throughout the world. His topics of instruction include Interviewing Children and Adolescents; Profiling and Interviewing Offenders; Child Abuse Investigations; and Domestic Violence and Its Effects on Children. Lt. Hertica has published articles on child abuse in *The Police Chief* magazine, the *FBI Law Enforcement Bulletin,* and the *APSAC Advisor.* He is Past President of the Board of Directors of the California Professional Society on the Abuse of Children and served on the Board of Directors of the American Professional Society on the Abuse of Children. He is a licensed marriage and family counselor. He currently works for 1736 Family Crisis Center, a domestic violence and youth shelter program in Redondo Beach, California.

CONTENTS

Preface

This program reflects the combination of our own experiences in the roles of counselor and police officer. Therefore, neither the manual nor the therapist's guide contain footnotes or references to other works. An introductory chapter accompanies the therapist's guide, citing some of the research and study that has taken place over the last twenty-five years that validates and supports our own perspective on family violence.

The manual provides an outline for you, the survivor, to assist you in evaluating your current, past, or future relationships in order that you may heal from and, later, avoid the destructive effects of domestic violence.

The manual is not the whole of your healing process; it is meant to be used during a process of growth and change in which you will also seek other avenues of information, guidance, and support. We encourage you to locate a therapist who has specific training in domestic violence, and who demonstrates an attitude of patience, compassion, and respect toward you. The therapist may have his or her own wishes for your future, but he or she must put these aside and, instead, assist you in developing your own goals. It is not the therapist's responsibility to make decisions for you or to take action for you. It is the therapist's responsibility to support you in your growth so that you can make your own decisions and take those actions that are right for you. The therapist provides information and resources, including referrals to other support systems such as self-help and therapy groups, law enforcement support, and legal services. The role of the therapist is to serve as a guide on your journey, helping you over the rough places on your path, and applauding when you successfully negotiate the twists and turns of your life journey.

Whatever the outcome of your work, it is our hope and wish that you will find this manual to be a companion that encourages you always to keep safe and value yourself.

Wendy Susan Deaton
Michael Hertica

Chapter 1

Is It Me?

- Are you in a relationship yet feeling isolated and alone?
- Do you believe that it is your fault if your partner is not happy?
- Do you believe that your partner only gets angry because he loves you?
- Do you believe your partner's criticisms are only meant to help you?
- Does your partner abuse you physically or emotionally?
- Do you feel there is danger to yourself or your children if you leave the relationship?
- Are you an emotional hostage?
- Do you fear that you cannot survive alone?
- Do you believe that if only you change, your partner will change?

*If your answer to any of these questions is yes,
then this book is for you.*

At times, everyone has had one or two of these thoughts, but if you are having such thoughts frequently, you may be a victim of domestic violence. As a victim, you may believe that you are responsible for causing or controlling everything that happens in the relationship. You may believe the problems in the relationship are your fault. You may rationalize, minimize, or explain away other reasons for your partner's behavior, and take on total responsibility for the violence. Taking responsibility gives you a feeling of power and control over situations that feel frightening and overwhelming. However, there are healthier ways to feel in control without trying to control the feelings, beliefs, and behavior of another person in a relationship.

WHAT IS DOMESTIC VIOLENCE?

Domestic violence includes physical violence, emotional abuse, economic abuse, sexual abuse, intimidation, and the use of children to gain power and control. Every relationship is unique and is composed of different kinds of behavior. A relationship can be abusive even without physical violence. Some relationships may involve only threats, blaming, and intimidation; some include only one kind of abusive behavior. Most abusive relationships, however, include several different kinds of harmful interactions.

Domestic violence can happen to anyone. It happens in families of every race, color, religion, and socioeconomic level. It happens to all ages, at all educational levels, and in same-sex relationships. Although some research studies suggest that abusive and violent behaviors occur more frequently at lower socioeconomic levels, having economic security or wealth does not protect anyone from abuse. Domestic violence does not happen only in other families; it could occur in yours. For ease in reading, we have used the female pronoun in talking about victims, but please remember that men can also be victims of domestic violence.

DEFINITIONS OF VIOLENCE IN RELATIONSHIPS

1. *Physical violence* includes pushing, throwing objects, hitting, kicking, or any other physical activity that can cause injury.
2. *Verbal and emotional abuse* includes making you feel badly about yourself, name-calling, making you think you have gone crazy, isolating you from friends and relatives, blaming you, and other kinds of "mind games."
3. *Economic abuse* includes making you financially dependent, keeping you from getting a job, or taking away your money or belongings.
4. *Sexual abuse* involves physical attacks on sexual parts of your body, or forcing you to have sex against your will.
5. *Intimidation* involves threatening, shouting, giving the silent treatment, or acting in a violent way in front of you by punching walls, breaking your personal things, or hurting your pets.

6. *Using children to gain power and control* involves threatening to take custody of your children; depriving your children of financial support; or making negative, untrue reports to the police, to social services, or to the courts.

These are not the only ways domestic violence can be expressed, but they are the most common things that happen. *If you have had some of these experiences, you need to continue to read this book.*

No easy fix exists for relationships; this is especially true for relationships that involve violence and abuse. If you are in a violent relationship, this book will not be the answer to all your problems. Instead, this book can serve as a friend and guide. It offers information about how you came into this relationship, how it is affecting you and your children, and how you can begin to make other, healthier choices in life. It will help you see the patterns of thinking, feeling, and behavior that have led you to choose this relationship, as well as the patterns that are harmful to you and those you love. This book will help you realize that there are different ways to view life, and that you have other options, and other choices you can make.

This book is for anyone who has ever been in a relationship that made you feel bad about yourself, in a relationship in which you didn't get the love or respect you deserve, or in which you were abused. It is also a book for professionals who work with people who have been or are currently in abusive relationships.

ACCEPTING WHERE YOU ARE

You are already taking the first step toward changing your life by reading this book. Reading this book means you are confronting the questions you have about your relationship and that you are concerned that your relationship is not healthy.

The next step in changing your life involves asking yourself some important questions:

- Are you ready to give up your denial and face the problem of violence in your relationship?
- Are you ready to admit that you are experiencing too much pain in your relationship, even if you are not ready to leave?

- Are you ready to accept that your relationship is having a negative effect on you and your children?
- Are you ready to accept that, even though physical violence is absent in your relationship now, the way things are going means that the threat of physical violence is growing?

Your history may have helped prepare you to be willing to be in unhealthy or unsafe relationships as an adult. Many adults who live in abusive or violent relationships first experienced some type of abuse or neglect in childhood. If you were abused as a child, you may have learned to believe that the abuse was your fault.

> Raelyn's father was physically and sexually abusive. When he hit or molested Raelyn, he told her she was being punished for being a "bad girl." He told her the abuse would stop only if she learned "how to behave." Raelyn believed her father. She believed that she was responsible for his behavior. As an adult, without understanding why, she was always seeking relationships in which she would receive approval for being a "good girl." Raelyn sought partners who reminded her of her father— partners who were abusive— and then she tried many different kinds of behavior to get them to stop abusing her. Because of her childlike belief system, Raelyn did not understand that the abuse was not the result of her behavior in the relationship, but instead was the result of choosing an abusive partner.

As a child you may have been taught that abuse is part of a normal relationship.

> Sherri grew up in a large extended family, with many uncles, cousins, and brothers. In Sherri's family, women were second-class citizens; they existed to serve men. Sherri's father and uncles made all the rules. Sherri could not have friends outside of school or visit the homes of other people. She did not have the chance to see that other families were not abusive. The women in Sherri's family were belittled, pushed, hit, and blamed for everything bad that happened. Sherri thought this was how all families operated— that being a victim was the normal role of a woman.

The child's brain is not fully developed. The stage of development of the child's brain causes the child to see the world differently than an adult sees the world. Children think that they are at the center of the world, rather than understanding that the world exists separately from them. Children do not understand that other people and other circumstances influence the events they experience. Experiences that support children's natural belief that they are the cause of everything are easily accepted, while experiences which show that their power and influence in the world are limited do not make sense to young children. Children's belief in their power over life events is very strong; therefore, it is easy to convince them that they are at fault for everything bad that happens.

If you grow up believing that you are at fault for your childhood abuse, or that abusive relationships are normal, you may carry these beliefs into adulthood. Childhood experiences are the most powerful of all experiences in shaping how you live as you grow up. What you learn in life after childhood may not seem to be as real or as true to you as your earliest experiences.

For example, imagine your baby self as a circle. Inside this circle is everything you experience in infancy—all your memories, thoughts, and feelings. From these experiences, you form a view of yourself and the world around you. Later experiences appear like rings around the original circle of beliefs, and everything that happens later is influenced by your earliest views.

If you are well loved and well cared for as a baby, you enter school and the social world expecting to be loved and cared for. You are attracted to people who are kind and caring, and who approve of you, because that is most familiar to you. If most of your early experiences are of pain, neglect, and rejection, you learn to expect negativity from others and you find yourself attracted to neglectful and abusive people, even though you do not like being hurt. Although you may have many positive interactions later in life, these experiences are not part of your core beliefs and they may never be as powerful in influencing your decisions as your earlier beliefs are. The earlier in life you come to some conclusion about who you are or how the world is, the more powerful that belief will be in shaping your future decisions, especially when it comes to choosing a partner.

Although as a child you may not have understood that you were not at fault for the abuse, as an adult, you can learn that you are never responsible for other's feelings, attitudes, or behavior, or for violence committed by them.

When you are a victim of abuse, as either a child or an adult, it is natural for you to make excuses for the other person's behavior. It is difficult to accept that the person you love, and who claims to love you, would hurt you. It is easier to rationalize and to try to find good reasons why the other person behaved in an unreasonable or hurtful way. It is easier to believe that it is your problem, your mistake, your fault; it must be that you are ignorant, stupid, or clumsy, just like your partner said. When you rationalize or make excuses for the other person and blame yourself instead, it is easier for you to go on loving and believing you are loved.

Making excuses for the other person and taking responsibility for the violence or the abuse is dangerous to you. This kind of thinking will eat away at your self-esteem and self-worth, causing you to lose respect for yourself. Thinking that you are at fault may mean that you do not try to protect yourself from dangerous behavior and that you will stay in a relationship that is unhealthy and unsafe for you.

You are not responsible for anyone else's behavior. Behavior is an individual choice, a conscious decision. And there is never a good excuse for someone to hurt you, emotionally or physically—no reason exists and no explanation is reasonable. You make excuses for your partner's behavior because this is what you have learned to do. When you make excuses, you avoid dealing with your fears about leaving and the confusion about how you will manage alone. You avoid accepting that your relationship is not going to work out. If you believe that the violent behavior results from something you are doing, you can continue to believe that changing your own behavior will change the behavior of your partner. Making excuses and taking the blame allows you to believe that you are in control and that you can change what is happening just by changing your own behavior.

You may try other ways to avoid facing the pain of admitting that your relationship is unsafe. Sometimes you can just forget, pretending that the violence never happened. You can forget what was actually said or done or how serious the danger was. If you can forget, then maybe it never happened and you can go on pretending, imagining, wishing, and hoping that all is well. This type of avoidance is called denial. Avoiding reality through denial is to live in a make-believe world. When you stay in denial, you fail to take the steps necessary to stay safe.

You may minimize the behavior, deciding that it is not as serious as it seems. You may think, "What he said really wasn't that hurtful. I am just too sensitive" or "He didn't really mean to hit me; he just was upset. It was an accident."

You cannot afford to minimize, rationalize, or deny. You especially cannot afford to forget. It is not safe for you to forget. You must remember what happened. Ultimately, you must let your memories come back, not to hurt or punish yourself, but as a way of facing reality and as a means to help you stay motivated to grow and change for the better. Accept that the violence is true. It did happen. And it has to stop.

As you begin to face what is happening to you, you will experience many feelings. It is natural to feel afraid, but you also will begin to feel the need to take action, to change your situation. This means you may have to end the relationship, which will likely have some important consequences. You may lose your home, the financial support provided by your partner, and the comfort of being married. You may fear that you will be unable to replace these things or that you will be unable to take care of yourself or your children. You may worry that you will not have enough money or a decent place to live. You may think you will never have another relationship, never again be loved, or that you will always be alone. Your fears are normal and natural, but usually they do not become reality. In most situations, when a person leaves an abusive relationship, she finds a way to support herself, she finds friends and professionals who can help, and—if she continues to grow and love herself—she finds another, healthier relationship. Fear is not a reason to stay in an unhappy, unhealthy, unsafe relationship.

Another feeling you may experience is anger. You may feel angry at yourself, at your partner, at people in your past, at friends or family members, or at professionals with whom you have worked. You may be afraid of your angry feelings because they remind you of the violence, but if you do not allow yourself to feel the anger, you will stay helpless and devastated. You may need help with your anger. A support group or a professional counselor can help you choose healthy ways of acknowledging and expressing your angry feelings without hurting yourself or anyone else. When you are working with your anger, remember that it is not your angry feelings that are harmful or dangerous, but the way that you express them. Anger does not have to spiral out of control; it does not have to cause harm to you or to others. Anger is part of the natural fight-or-flight response we all experience when faced with danger. Later in this book we offer some suggestions of constructive ways to deal with your anger.

If, when you face what is happening, you decide that you may have to end the relationship, you will, of course, feel sad and lonely. If you are honest with yourself, you will see that you have felt sad and lonely for a long time. No situation is as sad and as lonely as being with someone you love and not having your love returned. Do not mistake your sad and lonely feelings for a reason to stay in an unsafe relationship. Recognize that sadness and loneliness are normal reactions to the loss of any relationship.

You cannot wish away your sadness or loneliness, but you can express your feelings and get through them. Set time aside to deal with your feelings. If you feel like crying, go ahead and cry. The relationship didn't work out and you have a right to your feelings about it. Being sad does not mean you should stay in the relationship; being lonely now does not mean you will always be alone. Experience your feelings for a time, then set them aside and move on. If the feelings come back, go through this process again and again until you no longer feel the pain.

Finally, when you truly face that you are ready to take steps to stop the violence, you may feel a sense of relief and excitement. These feelings may embarrass you or make you uncomfortable. You may feel guilty because you are feeling happy that the relationship is ending. These feelings, too, are normal and natural. You feel relieved and excited because you are making healthy changes in your life that are going to bring better times to you and your children. If you do not feel relief and excitement at first, do not be concerned. These feelings will come when you are ready to allow yourself to be happy and free.

Chapter 2

Effects of Domestic Violence on the Victim

Certainly not all victims of domestic violence are women, but the highest percentage are. This chapter focuses on the effects on victims, which most often will be characterized as women. We acknowledge, however, that men can also be victims of domestic violence.

Many, if not all, victims of domestic violence use minimization, rationalization, denial, or forgetting to avoid facing the reality of their situation.

> Billie told her therapist, "Marco's only hit me once in three years of marriage." Later, however, she revealed that he kept his finances a secret from her and made her use her income for all the household expenses. They had sex only when he wanted to and this was mostly when he came home after drinking "with the boys." He yelled at her often, but she made a point of telling her therapist that Marco never yelled in front of, or hit, their son, Philipe. "I would leave him if he did," Billie stated forcefully. "My mom and dad went through worse than this and they are still together after thirty-five years." Billie did not see that she was in a classic domestic violence relationship. In fact, she believed, "Marco's the only man who ever really loved me."

Billie is a good example of how victims of violence minimize and rationalize their situation. Billie's motives for denying reality are obvious. She grew up in a family in which violence was accepted. To feel comfortable with her husband, she chose to believe that violence was a normal part of a relationship. Because she did not love herself in a healthy way, she could not imagine that anyone except Marco could find her lovable and desirable. By continuing to believe that Marco loved her, and by continuing to minimize and rationalize his violent behavior, Billie could stay "safely" married.

Most victims of domestic violence feel trapped and hopeless. Although they may have seen the violent situation developing for quite some time, often even before the marriage or before moving in with their partners, they do not know how to change or stop it. They are afraid to leave the relationship because they do not know how they will manage their children, their economic security, or their physical safety. They worry about what others will think if they separate—especially what their families will think. They do not feel confident about being able to meet their day-to-day needs. These fears and concerns lead them to stay in the violent situation even when their lives are at stake. They will often stay even after they finally recognize that they are unhappy and unsafe.

Domestic violence relationships take many forms. The relationship may contain all or only some of the following elements: jealousy, controlling behavior, unrealistic expectations, isolation, blaming behavior, cruelty, threats, sudden mood swings, and rigid gender (sex) roles.

ELEMENTS OF THE DYSFUNCTIONAL RELATIONSHIP

Jealousy

The violent partner is often jealous of everything and everybody in your life, including your work and even the children you have together. He may complain that you never spend enough time with him or that you never give him enough attention. He may accuse you of giving too much attention to other family members, to your friends, or to your hobbies, activities, or work. He often expresses his jealousy by first trying to reason with you, then by pouting, then by arguing, threatening, or trying to control you physically. He may follow or stalk you when you go out, secretly listen to your phone calls, and open your mail without your permission. He will not feel comfortable with anything you do that is not focused on him. Your partner may be capable of great persistence in his effort to possess you completely. He will try to wear you down so that eventually you will spend less and less time with other people and less time doing things that you enjoy or that are important to you. You may even quit your job in an effort to make your partner feel secure, but nothing you do will ever be enough.

Control

Domestic violence is about control. Your partner feels out of control inside, and he acts on his insecurity by trying to control you. He wants to control what you think and feel, where you go, who you see, what you do. Whenever he can, even in things that seem very unimportant, your partner may try to get you to do things and see things his way. He may ask you to change your hair, your makeup, or the way you dress, and then he may want you to change these things again. He may try to convince you that you do not understand finances or politics, and that you should let him make the decisions about how to spend the family money or how you should vote. He may become angry and assaultive when you try to act independently or when you want to make your own decisions, even when the decisions have nothing to do with him. In extreme cases, even decisions such as what you should eat for lunch may cause an argument.

Unrealistic Expectations

Your partner is likely to have very unrealistic expectations about how a relationship should be. He may believe that you should know what he wants and what he is thinking without him having to tell you. He may assume that you believe and feel exactly the same way he does about everything. If he feels like going out for chocolate ice cream, he thinks you must feel like going out for chocolate ice cream too. He may fear any differences or disagreements that you express. He may believe that you will go on giving in and putting up with his behavior no matter how outrageous and demanding he becomes.

Isolation

Your partner may want to separate you from other people and other activities that take away your attention. He may be outwardly controlling about your contact with others, or he may secretly and subtly try to undermine your trust and affection for people you know. He may lie to you about things your friends or family members have said and done, such as saying that your best friend made a pass at him, or that he heard your sister say she thought you were stupid. In time, his constant negative comments may cause you to distrust even those who are closest to you. When you cannot trust your parents, siblings, or best friends, you have only him to lean on, which is the way he likes it.

When a woman is exposed to this behavior and believes that she cannot get out, she begins to accommodate. She learns to tolerate the behaviors and to believe and adapt to the feelings that develop. Her accommodation allows the relationship to continue.

> Danielle was disturbed by some of Mitch's behaviors right from the beginning of their relationship. The very first night after they met he began to pester her for an exclusive commitment. Although she tried to resist his demand, eventually she gave in, hoping that her promise of exclusivity would help him feel secure enough to allow him to relax and enjoy the relationship. As soon as Danielle voiced her commitment, Mitch began complaining that she didn't spend enough time with him. He resented the time she spent with her friends and even the time she devoted to work and to her children. The arguments with Mitch started as heated debates, and at first Danielle held her ground and refused to give in to his complaints. Weeks went by and the fighting continued. In time, Danielle began to question herself. "Perhaps it is my problem," she thought. "Perhaps I'm not giving him enough attention." No matter how much time and energy Danielle put into the relationship, however, Mitch was never content. The arguments grew louder, longer, and more ugly. Soon Mitch was accusing Danielle of being cold and incapable of being a loving partner. In time, she began to believe that maybe he was right and that something was wrong with her. By the end of the first year of their relationship, Danielle had lost much of her sense of self-esteem and self-worth. She was isolated from her family and friends, and there was even a distance growing between herself and her children. Danielle no longer felt good about herself and she was constantly struggling to get approval from Mitch. Their fights now included Mitch holler-

ing, drinking, throwing things, and blaming her for his loss of control. Danielle was miserable and frightened, but she no longer felt strong enough to risk ending the partnership. She was caught in the trap of domestic violence by her early acceptance and accommodation of Mitch's unreasonable demands.

As the victim of domestic violence adjusts and accommodates, she begins to experience many painful feelings and symptoms of severe stress. These are some of the feelings and behaviors that victims of domestic violence report experiencing:

1. *Depression*—feelings of sadness, hopelessness, and helplessness. These are some of the things victims of domestic violence say about their depression:
   - "I can't remember how it felt to be happy."
   - "If I left, I would be alone and I couldn't stand that."
   - "There is nothing I can do."
   - "There is no way out. I made my bed; now I have to lie in it."
2. *Anxiety*—anxious feelings, inability to cope, always being on edge. These are some of the statements victims make about anxiety:
   - "I feel scared all the time. I can't sleep."
   - "I can't deal with life. I can't deal with anything anymore."
   - "I don't know why I am this way, but everything seems to bother me now."
3. *Sleep disturbances*—unable to sleep, nightmares, night terrors. This is how sleeplessness feels:
   - "I am always tired. I never feel rested."
   - "I don't want to close my eyes. I don't want to go through any more nightmares."
   - "Why can't I sleep like a normal person? There is something really wrong with me."
4. *Low self-esteem*—feelings of worthlessness, poor sexual self-image, thoughts of suicide, feelings of powerlessness. This is how worthlessness sounds:
   - "I don't know why he stays with me. I can't do anything right."
   - "I'm fat and ugly. No one else will want me."
   - "Maybe he and the children would be better off without me."

5. *Unrealistic expectations*—feelings that the partner can change, that by changing her own behavior, she can cause him to change. Here are some unrealistic expectations:
   - "When he gets his promotion, he will stop acting this way."
   - "I know I can make him happy. I just have to learn to do things the right way."
   - "He only acts this way because he loves me."
6. *Feelings of danger*—ever present feelings of danger to self and children. These are the feelings of danger:
   - "I can't be home late; he will be furious."
   - "I wish I could leave, but he would find me and it would just be worse."
   - "He will take away my children if I try to leave."
7. *Eating disorders*—bingeing, purging, overeating, etc. This is what happens when you have an eating disorder:
   - You eat even when you are not hungry because you are eating to feed your heart, not your stomach.
   - You start by eating just one cookie; suddenly you realize you have eaten the whole box of cookies.
   - You eat too much. You stick your finger down your throat and throw up. You still feel empty and sick. You want to eat again.

CYCLE OF VIOLENCE

There is a cycle to the violence in an abusive relationship. Initially, the relationship does not include violence. One reason many victims stay with abusive partners is that the violence has happened slowly and over a long period of time. The cycle is seductive (it tempts you) and escalating (gets worse over time). In the beginning it is hard to see that your partner's behavior is damaging and dangerous. The behavior becomes more and more violent as time goes by, often moving slowly from just pouting and arguing to shouting and blaming, to hitting walls, to pushing you, and, finally, to hitting you. By the time you realize that the relationship is violent, you are used to the abuse.

Margurite was thrilled when her handsome neighbor began trying to draw her attention. He was good-looking, charming, and had a very good job. Their first few dates were romantic and exciting. Within a week, Fernando began pressuring her for a commitment. The relationship seemed perfect at first. Then slowly, Margurite noticed Fernando was becoming possessive and demanding. She tried talking to him about her concerns and he agreed she was being reasonable and he would back off; but instead of the regular pressures he began pouting and picking at her about minor issues. She didn't want to spoil the relationship, so she did what she could to try to make him comfortable. Gradually, Margurite noticed that she and Fernando were arguing more and more. When they were not in a disagreement, however, everything was wonderful. It was several months into the relationship before Margurite first saw that Fernando had a temper. Angry at her for being late to a date with him, he shouted at her and punched the wall with his fist. His angry outburst frightened Margurite and she began to cry. Fernando quickly calmed down and began to smooth things over. Margurite thought his loss of control was just a one-time thing. She didn't see that it was the beginning of the cycle of violence.

Recognizing that a relationship is abusive is sometimes difficult because your partner is not angry and violent all the time. Every relationship has its own pattern of ups and downs. In some relationships, violent outbursts occur daily or weekly. In others, the violence occurs infrequently. With some partners, years can go by between blowups. Infrequent explosions make it particularly hard for the victim to break free; during each lull in the violence, she believes that the cycle has finally ended.

As the batterer goes through the cycle of violence, his behavior changes. These changes in behavior may confuse you. The cycle begins with a buildup of stress in the relationship. It may start simply as a feeling of tension or discomfort when you are with your partner.

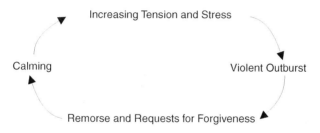

Increasing Tension and Stress

Calming

Violent Outburst

Remorse and Requests for Forgiveness

Then there is a period of criticism, blame, yelling, and intimidation. Nothing you do is right and whatever is "wrong" is all your fault. The harder you try to "correct" what is wrong, the more you are blamed. The stress continues to build until there is an explosion.

During the violent phase of the cycle, some kind of physical violence occurs. The batterer may have a tantrum, throw things, break things, punch walls, or push, kick, or punch you. It is at this point that you are the most frightened. Sometimes others hear the explosion and the police are called. During the outburst you may think about leaving, about getting out. You may realize that you don't deserve this punishment, that you don't have to live under this kind of stress. You may develop a plan for leaving or you may even leave, temporarily.

After the explosion, however, your partner expresses sorrow and remorse for what has happened. He seems to come to his senses suddenly and promises he will never be violent again. His request for forgiveness rekindles your dream that things can change, that the relationship can get better. Promises and reassurances of love cause you to hesitate about ending the relationship. Suddenly, you have hope again. You want to give him one more chance; after all, you truly love him. You decide to try again. You move from the "forgiveness" phase to the calming or honeymoon phase of the cycle of violence. However, without help or intervention in the form of consequences and counseling, your honeymoon will only last a short time. Eventually, stress will start building and the cycle will repeat itself.

The stress that triggers the domestic violence cycle is out of your control. Some of the stress comes from conditions in the home or in the relationship, but stressors also arise from other situations in your partner's life, such as his work environment or financial pressures, or internally, from old, unresolved traumas and emotions. Your partner's reactions, similar to yours, involve learned behavior from the past. If your partner did not have the opportunity to learn constructive ways to express his irritations and frustrations, violence may seem a natural way for him to vent his anger.

The cycle of violence is predictable and will continue to occur despite your best efforts. Everyone in your family system must participate if the cycle is to be broken. The first step is for you to recognize that you do not cause, and cannot control, your partner's behavior. If you have children, you want to serve as a role model for them. You want to reduce the opportunity for faulty learning for your children by setting good boundaries against unhealthy or destructive behavior. You want your children to understand, however, what they can control and what they cannot. You must teach them the same lessons you need to learn, i.e., that you do not cause, control, or cure someone else's violent behavior.

In Chapter 3, we will talk more about how your children are affected by domestic violence and how you can help them avoid learning unhealthy relationship behaviors.

Living with domestic violence eventually destroys your self-esteem, self-worth, and self-confidence. If you are constantly criticized, blamed, intimidated, or physically treated disrespectfully through pushing, shoving, kicking, hitting, or forced sex, eventually you will come to believe that you are not very lovable, not worthwhile, not important, and not valuable. If you believe that something about you or what you are doing is causing the abuse, then your self-esteem and self-worth will definitely be negatively affected by what is happening to you.

Since the cycle of violence and your partner's behavior are out of your control, eventually you are likely to begin to lose confidence in your ability to manage your life. As you begin to feel helpless about controlling the violence, you may also begin to question your ability to control other aspects of your life. Because your decisions and actions are always being questioned and criticized, you will soon begin to doubt yourself. You may also lose confidence in your ability to make decisions about how to dress, how to spend money, how to raise your children, how to behave with your friends or other family, or even how to conduct yourself on the job.

The loss of self-esteem, self-worth, and self-confidence makes it harder for you to see clearly that you are capable of ending the relationship and surviving. With low self-esteem and poor self-worth you will question whether anyone else could ever love you, whether you could ever find another relationship. The thought of being alone for a lifetime may be just too depressing and too frightening to face. You may believe that staying in this unhealthy relationship is better than no relationship at all.

The loss of self-confidence, especially if it extends to your job or your career, also supports your staying in your unhealthy relationship. It may feel too overwhelming, too difficult, to make the hard decisions necessary for leaving. You may find that even if you want to leave, you have difficulty figuring out how you will pay for things, where you will live, or how you will manage the children. Often you will stay in the relationship simply because you can no longer see that you have the option to leave.

> Mary was a successful physical therapist with her own business when she met Richard, a patient with a serious knee injury. Although he was married, Richard and Mary eventually became romantically involved; two years later, he left his wife. Mary never thought of Richard as controlling; instead she interpreted his constant criticisms as his way of helping her grow, and his endless demands as a reflection of how much he needed and loved her. As the months went by, Mary devoted more and more of her time and energy to trying to make Richard happy and to taking care of his worries, needs, desires, work, children, problems, and pain. Even when Richard began waking Mary up in the middle of the night to listen to his worries and massage away the pain in his leg, she put aside her resentment and made excuses for him. Several years after their relationship began, Mary developed a serious health problem. Her business dissolved because she was unable to be at work regularly. Her friends and family members also drifted away, expressing to Mary as gently as they could that Richard made them feel unwelcome. When Mary was hospitalized with breast cancer, a social worker came to see her and tried to help Mary see that she was being swallowed up by the relationship. Although Richard was not physically violent, his constant criticisms and his endless emotional demands had destroyed Mary's self-confidence as surely as a fist in her face. Now breast cancer had taken the last of Mary's self-esteem. She felt totally dependent upon Richard financially and emotionally. She couldn't imagine anymore how she could exist without him. Whatever behavior Richard displayed in the future, Mary would never leave him now.

The batterer's emotional and verbal abuse of you is intended to destroy your positive feelings so that you will be unable to leave. Internally, he is a person who feels insecure and inferior. He feels frightened and overwhelmed when you are strong, competent, and happy with yourself; therefore, he attacks your strengths. As you feel worse about yourself, your partner feels stronger, but he also feels more angry because now he cannot respect you. These reactions work together in a vicious cycle that contributes to the violence.

You may find that the values and beliefs you were taught as a child about marriage, loyalty, and commitment are in conflict with your desire or need to leave your relationship. The reactions of other members of the family and your religious beliefs may also cause you to think that leaving is not an option. Family and religious values are important factors in any decision you make about a relationship, and it is appropriate to consider them, along with all the other factors; however, it is also important that you do not use an ideal system of values to avoid facing the responsibility you have to keep yourself safe.

If you are in a relationship with a batterer, it is essential that you recognize that nothing you do, including allowing your confidence and worth to be destroyed, will change the situation. The violence can end only if your partner, on his own, recognizes the problem and decides for his own reasons to get help.

Chapter 3

Effects of Domestic Violence on Children

HOW CHILDREN DEVELOP UNDER STRESS

In the normal course of child development, the child's internal biological energy moves naturally from the first tasks of survival to more complex and sophisticated tasks. Infants, for example, first learn to regulate their ability to feed and to sleep in a regular pattern. They gradually become aware of themselves as an interesting item of study and also slowly begin to relate to their surroundings and to others around them. If children grow in a secure environment, their development unfolds naturally. They feel safe to become mobile, to sit up, crawl, walk, and, eventually, run. They learn to communicate and, eventually, to separate from the protection of their parents or caretakers to test their strengths and skills in an effort to make a place for themselves in the world.

Infant who grow up with stress, tension, and turmoil cannot focus on their development in a normal way. Much of their energy must be used to try to understand, deal with, and protect themselves from the frightening events around them. Their adjustment to the world may be delayed or distorted and their normal course of development interrupted.

Infants

As has been mentioned, domestic violence has a dramatic effect on children. This can and does start as early as when the child is in the womb. As many as 50 percent of pregnant women in abusive relationships are struck even though they are pregnant.

Even if born healthy, children living with domestic violence start life at risk physically, mentally, emotionally, and spiritually. During infancy, these children may experience difficulties bonding as the mother tries either to distance herself from the children so they do not stand in the "line of fire," or keep her children too close to her in an effort to protect herself from the violence. The mother may use her children as a shield, believing that she will not be abused if she is holding a child. Unfortunately, once physical violence has begun, most mothers find that infants provide them no protection and, instead, their actions put their children at risk.

Other risks to infants in a scene of domestic violence include disruptions in feeding and sleeping schedules, lack of consistent nurturing, and risk of injury if the children are shaken, dropped, hit by a thrown object, or deliberately assaulted. All of these risks pose a threat to children's normal development.

Preschool Age

Preschool children carry the effects of domestic violence into all areas of their lives. They may suffer from sleep disturbances such as nightmares and night terrors where they wake up screaming, absolutely terrorized by their dreams. They may feel confusion and insecurity that they express through regressive behaviors such as thumb-sucking, clinging, or bed-wetting after they have been potty trained.

During the preschool years, children will internalize the behaviors that they witness, beginning the process of faulty learning. This stage of children's cognitive (mental) development causes them to believe that they are at the center of the world and responsible for everything; therefore, the violence is their fault. Also consistent with their natural development, children may identify with the same-sex parent. Often, a boy will model himself after the male in the family (usually the aggressor) while a girl will learn the woman's role (usually the victim).

Elementary School Years

When they came to the shelter, Juan, nine, and Maria, ten, were a handful. Their attention spans were short and when they got upset or frustrated, Juan became violent and Maria egged him on. The other kids were afraid. Whenever staff attempted to correct their behavior and set boundaries and consequences, their mother tried to rescue them, as she had always done with their father. Mother initially blamed the shelter and the other kids there for being a bad influence. She said that their behavior was much worse there than it had been at home. She didn't realize that in the shelter, they felt safe enough to act out their fear and anger.

During the school years, the behavior of boys will often continue to differ from that of girls based on this identification with their same-sex parent. Their behavior is called gender specific; that is, boys will generally demonstrate different attitudes and behaviors from girls. Boys more often act out, or externalize, the stress they are experiencing, while girls more often keep in, or internalize, their pain and stress. This means that boys who have lived with domestic violence frequently engage in aggressive behaviors, including fighting, disobedience at home and at school, and destruction of property, while girls are more likely to be depressed, anxious, and withdrawn and to complain of physical ailments such as stomachaches and headaches. These gender roles, however, are not so rigid as to exclude either sex from exhibiting some of the behaviors common to the other sex. Girls can act out and boys can have stomachaches. Unfortunately, because of their aggressive behavior, the boys often attract most of the attention, leaving the girls, who are also suffering, largely ignored.

School problems also begin to arise at this time. These children may be so concerned about what is happening at home that they cannot concentrate on the learning process. Social development is affected as the child, who has not learned constructive methods of resolving conflicts, is confused about interpersonal boundaries and may be over- or underinvested in friendships, unable to relax with the normal ebb and flow of relating. Some children, on the other hand, may flee from their problems by focusing intensely on their school experience, both academic and social.

Academic Interference

Normal school development can be dramatically affected by domestic violence in a number of specific ways:

1. School may be missed to stay home to protect the mother.
2. Homework may be missed due to an inability to concentrate at home, especially during tension-building and outburst phases of violence.
3. Children may fall asleep in class because they are afraid to fall asleep at home during bedtime hours for fear they or their mother may be hurt while they sleep. This, in addition to nightmares and night terrors, may cause the child to be tired or to fall asleep in class. These problems can result in loss of academic progress, poor grades, low self-esteem, and more problems at home.

Social Interference

Children from violent families do not want to bring their friends home. They have trouble learning how normal social interactions work, experience problems establishing trusting relationships, and have difficulty recognizing threatening situations. Some children become "parentified"; that is, they grow up too fast trying to assume the role of the adult and the parent in the family in an attempt to care for the parent who is being abused or to protect their younger siblings. These children are especially at risk for injury from accidents, harm in unrecognized danger situations, and suicide attempts.

Adolescents

> Mark spent a lot of time alone with his father working on fixing their house. When his older sister, Riley, expressed her frustration about Mark not helping to try to protect their mother from their father's assaults, Mark explained that he was afraid to intervene, afraid that he would then pay for it when he and his father were alone. Both Mark and Riley told friends that they never wanted to have children; they never wanted a child to be afraid the way they were afraid.

The teen years are the time when children seek independence. Adolescents who are exposed to domestic violence, however, may not have the skills to handle this phase of life successfully because of earlier disruptions in their development. A number of different responses may be used by the adolescent challenged by life at this time.

Because things are so difficult at home, adolescents who have lived with domestic violence may seek surrogate families (gangs or groups of drug and alcohol abusers, etc.) where they feel accepted. These friendships can lead to aggressive, antisocial, or criminal behavior and even more difficulties adjusting at home and at school. Even if a surrogate family is not sought out, antisocial behavior may occur (stealing, substance abuse, school disturbances) as a way for adolescents to draw attention to themselves. Even negative attention is better than no attention. Suicide is also a concern in some of these situations.

Based on what teens have experienced in their families, they are vulnerable to abusive relationships. Violence in the relationship seems normal; some teens even believe that the expression of violence is a demonstration of love. Victims may again believe that an abusive relationship is better than no relationship. Date rape, which goes largely unreported, is not uncommon.

Adolescents who act out violently usually believe that violence is an appropriate form of conflict resolution and a way to gain respect and control. Some believe violence can be explained away if there is a reason or excuse, such as drinking or some other provocation.

The Emotional Effect of Violence on Children

Children who witness domestic violence may experience all the same painful emotions and symptoms of stress that are felt by the direct victims. Children may become depressed, develop anxiety or sleep disorders, or develop feelings of unworthiness. Many children feel helpless, powerless, and without hope for the future, while others feel angry and full of rage. Some children generalize their experiences at home and begin to see or sense danger everywhere. They become withdrawn, suspicious, or even paranoid. Children can develop eating disorders, begin acting out sexually, or start using drugs and alcohol to escape the fear and pain they feel as a result of the family violence.

Your children want and need you to protect them from the violence and to provide a model of a strong, healthy adult by taking care of yourself and them, and, if necessary, by leaving the relationship.

The bad news for children growing up in violent households is that they can suffer emotional, physical, academic, or social problems. The good news is that children are amazingly resilient. With the proper help, children can recover from the effects of domestic violence and learn better ways of relating to others.

Chapter 4

The Batterer

Chan was handsome, charming, and intelligent. He had a stable job with a good income and was raising a young son on his own. Maureen thought she had finally found the man of her dreams. For the first several weeks everything was perfect; then the arguments began. Chan felt neglected: Maureen didn't spend enough time with him and didn't pay enough attention to him. He distrusted her, pressuring her for an exclusive commitment, even wanting to set a wedding date. Several times over the next few months, Maureen tried to end the relationship. Chan's constant demands were wearing her down. He had also begun to say upsetting things to her, attacking her character, making her feel guilty and inadequate. Within a day after each attempted breakup, Chan was back, begging forgiveness, promising to change. A year went by and the arguments became louder, longer, and more destructive. Still, whenever Chan sought to reestablish the relationship, Maureen would give in. "I know our fighting is not good," she stated, "but I just have to help Chan feel secure. It isn't as if our relationship is really violent, after all. It isn't as though he hits me or anything like that!"

Many things kept Maureen in the relationship despite Chan's problems with insecurity and anger. She was attracted to him, he had a responsible job, and he seemed like a good father. Most of all, Maureen was impressed by Chan's determination to keep pursuing her. She thought, "He loves me so much. Look what he puts up with and still he keeps coming back!"

Maureen did not understand that she was already caught in a domestic violence cycle. Although Chan had not yet used physical violence, the couple's fighting was already affecting Maureen's self-esteem and self-confidence. It was highly likely, also, from the increased frequency and intensity of their fights, that physical violence would occur if the relationship continued.

There is no single profile of an abuser, nor any one single reason for a batterer to do what he does. You cannot identify a batterer when you meet him; he looks like any other person—your friend, neighbor, doctor, brother, even yourself.

The cycle of domestic violence is intergenerational; that is, for the most part, the pattern of violent behavior in the home is learned from a home where violence is experienced. Batterers have learned that through threats, intimidation, and violence they can gain control of the household. The lessons of domestic violence are learned through both witnessing and experiencing. In some families, only selected members, such as the mother or the mother and the female children, are battered. In other families, boys also may be criticized, degraded, humiliated, hit, kicked, or punched. In some families, everyone—from grandparents to children—is at risk for being abused.

Inside himself, the abuser is a frightened and insecure individual overwhelmed with feelings of inferiority, anxiety, depression, and unresolved rage. These powerful feelings cause the batterer to live daily with a sense of helplessness and powerlessness. Like the victim, the batterer feels confused and frightened, unable to consider a variety of options. When upset, he reacts impulsively, asserting himself in aggressive ways to try to control his environment and the people around him. Without intervention, these controlling, abusive behaviors will continue and may even get worse.

Batterers are found in all socioeconomic, racial, ethnic, educational, and age groups. Although women can be violent, the majority of batterers are men. Some batterers seem easy to recognize, as they always seem angry and unpredictable, but others may appear perfectly "normal" in their daily behavior, only erupting under stressful circumstances. All batterers, whatever their style, are equally dangerous.

Some of the more common behavior patterns that are seen in batterers include the following:

- In the beginning of the relationship, there is a push for an immediate, intense involvement. He jumps into plans for the future when no solid foundation has yet been established for the relationship.

- As the relationship continues, he demonstrates poor impulse control; his temper and anger are unpredictable.
- Excessive jealousy is expressed and accusations are made against you. He attempts to control your activities and your contact with other people. He invades your privacy, opens your mail, listens to your phone messages, and even goes through your personal property.
- He tries to isolate you from your family and friends, claiming his company should satisfy you totally.

The abuser has a variety of mental and emotional defense mechanisms that help him justify his behavior. He blames others for failures and problems, using rationalization, minimization, projection, and denial to explain his actions and relieve himself of responsibility for his behavior. As long as the batterer can maintain his belief that his violent behavior is justifiable and excusable, he is unable to effect any change in his actions.

- He maintains rigid sex roles and may be forceful during sex.
- He is physically and verbally cruel to children, animals, and to you.
- He often abuses alcohol or other substances.

You may see other behaviors that are dangerous; however, the behaviors listed here are the most common.

Men who are abusive often consider their partners and their children as their possessions, expecting them to fulfill certain "roles" and to behave in specific ways. The abuser becomes upset at interference from outsiders, including family, friends, or authorities such as the police or the court. The abuser believes it is his right to control his family, set expectations, and issue discipline as he sees fit, without outside intervention. Many batterers have their beliefs reinforced when victims, neighbors, or friends call the authorities and the authorities fail to take positive action. After several incidents of involvement with the authorities where no consequences have been given, the batterer may start to feel safe from outside intervention.

Whatever the cause of aggression, whether genetic, learned, or related to substance abuse, change is unlikely to occur unless the batterer experiences serious consequences for his behavior. Battering behavior is generally learned early in life and is, therefore, associated with intense, primitive emotions that to the abuser honestly feels are out of his control. The following comments were heard in a batterers' group:

- "It's the bitch's fault. I gave her everything but nothing was ever good enough. She always wanted more and kept bitching at me. I wouldn't have hit her if she hadn't pushed me."
- "It's the cops' fault. They came out and didn't even listen to me. They took her side. They've been out plenty of times before and nothing ever happened."
- "If I could've afforded a lawyer I wouldn't have been convicted. The PD [public defender] doesn't care. Everyone just believes the woman. What about my rights?"

For change to occur, the batterer must have some insight into the inappropriateness of his actions. He must be capable of understanding that instead of achieving the security, love, and attention he needs, his possessiveness, jealousy, and violence destroy his loved ones and drive them to resentment, rejection, and even hatred. In most cases, change will only occur when the abuser realizes that the potential loss is greater than the rewards he experiences from his abusive behavior.

It is possible for a natural, unrelated traumatic event, such as a serious illness in the family, an accident, or death of a loved one to trigger a sense of awareness and insight that motivates the batterer to evaluate his behavior. Other consequences, such as having his wife and family leave, being arrested, or causing irrevocable harm to someone he cares about can also influence an effort to change. Unfortunately, without natural, emotional, or legal consequences, the batterer has no reason to change.

Many batterers find that their problems with attitudes and behavior become bigger as a result of substance abuse. A strong parallel exists between the abuse of alcohol and drugs and domestic violence. Family members may report that violence occurs only when the batterer is drinking or using drugs, or when he is suffering the tension of untreated withdrawal from chemical dependency. It is important to recognize, however, that drug and alcohol abuse do not cause abusive behavior. They are merely used as rationalizations for it. The issues of substance abuse and chemical dependency must addressed for change to be meaningful and lasting. The batterer cannot evaluate his behavior or bring change into his life unless he is clean and sober for a significant period of time. Participation in an alcohol and drug program and membership in Alcoholics Anonymous (AA) or Narcotics Anonymous (NA) are important parts of overcoming violent behavior.

Chapter 5

What You Can Do

A violent relationship is a danger to your physical, mental, emotional, and spiritual survival. Although you may love your partner, you must understand that your love cannot change, control, or cure his violent behavior. You deserve to live free of the threat of violence.

Many victims of domestic violence remain with the batterer because of low self-esteem and poor self-worth. That is, some victims may come to love the batterer more than they love themselves. They may come to believe that he is more important, his needs must be met, and his life is more worthwhile. This is an unhealthy, dangerous perspective. In a healthy relationship, partners love themselves equally as much as they love each other.

Loving yourself does not mean being selfish, self-centered, or uncaring. It simply means that your safety, security, happiness, and well-being deserve your attention. It means you have the right to live free of the violence brought about by your partner's internal pain and insecurity.

Many couples who experience marital conflict use family or couples counseling to resolve their differences. Couples who experience violence as a part of their marital conflict may also believe they can get help through counseling. Unfortunately, family and couples counseling have been found not to be useful for families in which there is violence. In couples and family counseling, the relationship is viewed as the focus, and the violence is seen only as a symptom. During counseling, it is often difficult for the abused person to be open and honest in front of the abuser. She may fear, quite realistically, that after the session, the abuser will strike back with violence for things that were revealed during the session. Also, because the counseling is directed at maintaining the relationship, the woman may be viewed as being partly responsible for the violence. This approach, viewing the victim as partly responsible for the abuse, may serve only to reinforce the abuser's belief that his behavior is reasonable and acceptable. Although couples counseling may have some value for couples in which both individuals are serious about working on the relationship, it is likely to be helpful only later on in the counseling process after other types of therapy have brought about the necessary changes in both the victim's and the abuser's attitudes toward power and control.

Abusers can benefit from individual therapy, but even individual therapy has limitations. In individual therapy, abusers may be allowed to focus on ways to handle or manage their anger, while the underlying causes of their problems with anger and aggression, such as faulty learning and other family of origin issues, are minimized or ignored. In individual therapy, the abuser has the opportunity to manipulate and shape the therapist's view of his current family life. Without checking in with other family members, the therapist has no way to know if the abuser is honestly changing his behavior.

Individual therapy can be an important influence in recovery from domestic violence, but to be effective it must be viewed as only one part of a larger system approach to the problem. Individual therapy, for both batterer and victim, should always include a detailed review of the individual's childhood and previous relationship histories.

A complete approach for the abuser in a domestic violence situation will include the following components:

1. Criminal and civil accountability for the batterer
2. Protection and support for women and children during the course of batterer's treatment
3. Treatment for substance abuse and chemical dependency, including continued membership in AA or NA
4. Group therapy for the abuser (In group therapy, the abuser is confronted by others like himself, others with whom he can identify and who know all the ways in which he tries to avoid accepting responsibility for his behavior. Group confrontation has the power to break through emotional defenses and denial in a way that individuals, whether family, friends, or therapists, cannot do.)
5. Group therapy for the victim (In group therapy, the victim is given support and practical guidance on how to protect herself and her children. Her isolation is broken and she has the chance

to look at the destructive perceptions and beliefs that have developed as a result of the abuser's influence.)

6. Group therapy for the children (In group therapy, the children are
reassured that the violence in the home is not their fault. Members
of the group share the fear, hurt, and rage that has resulted from
the violence, and each child learns that this family is not the only
family to experience these difficulties. The children are also edu-
cated on how to manage their own insecurities and anger and how
to keep themselves safe from the violence in the home.)

7. Individual therapy for the abuser (In individual therapy, the
abuser can explore the roots of his violent behavior. He can
examine the crises or traumas from childhood that have caused
his anger, and he can learn about his perceptions and learned behaviors. This will help him build a sense of inner security and
self-confidence and develop skills for managing destructive behaviors.)

8. Individual therapy for the victim (In individual therapy, the victim can resolve her old crisis and trauma, learn new patterns of
behavior, and rebuild self-esteem, self-worth, and confidence.)

9. Child therapy (In individual and sibling therapy, the children of
violent families can express their feelings through play, art,
movement, and talk. Therapy lets the children resolve current
fears and concerns, develop anger management tools, and learn
methods of self-protection. The children's therapist can help the
children understand that adult violence is not their fault and can
help to empower the children to keep themselves safe.)

When therapy does not work or is not the answer, other solutions
must be found. The fact is that unless something is done, the relationship is not likely to improve. Many will ask the question, "Why doesn't
she just leave?" But most victims in relationships know that the solu-
tion is not that easy. Here are some suggestions for what you can do
when therapy is not the answer.

Learn about the resources in your community. All communities
have some type of hotline for getting information about domestic violence. The workers on these hotlines are used to handling violent situations and can provide you with ideas and resources. They can refer
you to agencies and programs that will assist you. Most communities
also have shelters that will house you and your children should you

decide to leave. It will help you to know that you do not have to stay in a dangerous or painful relationship. You have other choices. *Memorize the hotline phone number.*

Learn how the laws on domestic violence work in your community. You may be able to get help through the police or the courts, using emergency protective orders, restraining orders, or other legal instruments. These orders may help protect you, but remember that a piece of paper is only that. A restraining order will do no good unless you are willing to enforce it and to call for help when you feel you are unable to protect yourself.

Have a safety plan. This is of critical importance. If you do decide to leave, you need a plan. More women are hurt during the process of leaving than at any other time in the relationship. Without a plan, the chances of being hurt are increased. Many women who do leave soon return, and they may leave several times before they finally stay away. Although this pattern of leaving and returning may be discouraging, do not give up. It is not easy to break the patterns of a lifetime. Leave as often as you need to, until you can stay away for good. Be as clear as you can about what makes you leave and what makes you return. Being honest with yourself is an important part of the growing process.

SAFETY PLANS

Safety During an Explosive Incident

1. If an argument seems unavoidable, try to go to a room or area that is near an exit. Try to avoid bathrooms and kitchens or other places where there are weapons. In the bathroom, the water, hair dryers and hair curlers, tile floors, and the hard porcelain fixtures may be used as weapons. Also, bathrooms usually have only one exit and do not allow a quick or easy escape. Even if it has a backdoor, the kitchen is dangerous because it contains access to fire for burning, water for drowning, and knives, forks, blenders, and other items that can be used to cause harm.
2. Practice getting out of your home safely. Identify the path that will get you out of the house and to safety the most quickly.
3. Have a bag packed and keep it in an undisclosed but handy place, such as at a friend's house. With a packed bag, you will not have

to take the time to locate important items, thereby giving the batterer the opportunity to talk you out of leaving—or for you to talk yourself out of leaving.

4. Find a neighbor whom you can tell about the violence and ask this person to call the police if he or she hears a disturbance at your house.

5. Develop a code word to use with your children, family friends, and neighbors to let them know when you need the police.

6. Plan where you will go if you must leave home, even if you think you won't ever really need to leave.

7. Use your own instincts and judgment wisely. If the situation is very dangerous, consider giving the abuser what he wants to calm him down and wait for a better time to leave. You have the right to do whatever is necessary to protect yourself and your children until you are out of danger.

Safety When Preparing to Leave

1. Open a savings account in your own name to give you financial independence. Think of other ways you can increase your independence.

2. Leave money, an extra set of keys, copies of important papers, and extra clothes with someone you trust so you can leave quickly.

3. Decide who would be able to let you stay with them or lend you some money. Don't tell anyone else who your safety person is.

4. Keep a shelter phone number close at hand. Memorize it.

5. Review your safety plan as often as possible. When the time comes to leave, you may not be able to think clearly and you need to be able to act automatically. Map out and practice your plan when you are calm and can think clearly.

> *Remember that the most dangerous time*
> *is when you are leaving.*

Safety in Your Own Home

1. If the abuser leaves the home, change the locks on your doors as soon as possible. Buy additional locks and safety devices to secure your windows.

2. Discuss a safety plan with your children for when you are not with them.
3. Inform your children's school, day care, and baby-sitters, etc., about who has permission to pick up your children, and who is not allowed access to your children.
4. Inform neighbors and your landlord that your partner no longer lives with you and that they should call the police if they see him near your home.

Safety with a Protective Order

1. Find out what protective orders are available to you. To do this, you might try calling your local district attorney's office, victim-witness office, attorney service, or police department.
2. Keep your protective order on you at all times. In many communities, if you have a protective order and you call the police, they must come as soon as possible. Without a protective order, you may have a difficult time getting help when you need it.
3. Call the police if your partner breaks the order in any way, by writing, calling, or coming to your home or work. Do not wait for the situation to become violent before calling for help.
4. Inform friends and family that you have a protective order. Insist that they agree to help protect you from your partner. This means that they do not carry messages asking for forgiveness and do not let the abuser think his behavior is okay with them. Most of all, they do not tell him where to find you. Give a copy of your order to a friend, family member, or therapist.
5. Be smart; remember, a protective order will not prevent you from being harmed.

Safety on the Job and in Public

1. Decide who at work you will tell about your situation. Always tell office or building security.
2. Vary your routine. Try to arrange to arrive at and leave work at different times and by different routes.
3. Make a safety plan for when you leave work. Have someone escort you to your car or bus. Think about what you would do if

something happened to you while going home so that you will be prepared to respond to any emergency.

Your Safety and Emotional Health

1. If you are thinking about returning to a potentially abusive situation, discuss an alternate plan with someone you trust and respect.
2. If you have to communicate with your partner, do so in the safest way possible, in a public place around other people who have agreed to help protect you. *Never* agree to get in a car with the abuser, never go to an apartment or house or private office with him, and never go to an isolated beach or park. Even if you believe things are in control and you can handle him, *never* put your safety at risk.
3. Practice having positive thoughts about yourself and being assertive with others about your needs. You need to rebuild your self-esteem and self-confidence.
4. Seek counseling for yourself and your children. Include victim support groups.
5. Decide whom you can talk to freely and openly to give you the support you need to stay safe.

What to Take If You Leave

- Identification
- Children's birth certificates
- Bank book
- Checkbook
- Protective order
- Medications
- School records
- Social Security cards

- Driver's license
- Money
- Your birth certificate
- Insurance papers
- Deed, lease, rental agreement
- Address books
- Jewelry
- Work permits

- Green cards   • Welfare identification

- Passport   • Divorce papers

- Small children's toys   • House and car keys

- Personal pictures or possessions
  that are precious to you

The preparations you make before you leave can mean the difference between staying safe and putting yourself in danger. Good preparations can help you to feel confident and in control, so that you can be successful in getting free.

Chapter 6

After You Leave

You have finally gathered together the courage and the resources to leave your abusive relationship and now you wonder what lies ahead for you. At first you may have many fears and worries.

- Will he stay away?
- Can you stay away?
- Will you be able to make it on your own?
- What will happen when he wants to see the children?

In time, you may feel relieved and energized, even excited, because you have finally broken the pattern of abuse. Eventually, you will begin to grieve the loss of your relationship. Your grief will involve many different emotions at different times. It is appropriate to grieve the loss of your relationship, even though you recognize that ending the relationship was the right thing to do. You are grieving for the love you had, the love you thought you had, or the love and happiness you hoped to create. You are grieving because the relationship didn't work out. You are grieving the death of your dream, of the fairy tale that didn't come true. You need to allow yourself plenty of time and space to experience all your emotions. This is a time to grieve and a time to heal. You will heal as you allow yourself to live through your grief.

> It took Marianna fourteen years to finally leave her abusive husband. For a long time, Marianna thought that once she finally got up the courage to leave, she would feel fine. After all, she had spent years grieving the loss of the relationship that she wanted to have with her husband. Even though she was concerned about her financial security and about dealing with her ex-husband's visits with the children, she had not worried at all about her emotional reaction. Shortly after the breakup, Marianne was surprised and

upset to find herself missing her husband. She noticed that she was thinking about all the good things and that the memories of the unhappy times and the violent times were fading. About seven months after the breakup, Marianne noticed that she was missing her ex-husband more than ever. Marianne shared her feelings with her counselor who helped her to identify that this period of time also marked what would have been her fifteenth wedding anniversary. The counselor helped Marianne to remember the reasons that had led to her decision to leave. He also reframed Marianne's feelings, helping her to see that these feelings were nostalgic memories, the memories that she would, of course, want to keep. But he stated that these memories were only a part of the picture and that the memories and feelings that she was experiencing were not a reason to return to the abusive relationship. Marianne allowed herself to recognize that she needed more time to grieve the end of her marriage. It was okay for her to be sad, and normal for her to feel lonely. By acknowledging and working with her feelings, she was soon able to move through the feelings and accept that the end of the relationship was the best thing for her. As her grief began to ease, Marianne noticed that, for the first time since the breakup, she could think about her ex-husband with neither hateful nor yearning feelings. She began to notice that there were other attractive men around her; she felt flattered when a man at work began to pay her special attention. Although she was not yet ready for another partnership, Marianne recognized that, finally, she was truly letting go and outgrowing her abusive relationship.

BUILDING A RELATIONSHIP WITH YOURSELF

In time, you will move past shock, sadness, anger, and relief and you will begin to worry about the future. You are concerned about being alone and being lonely. You wonder if you can ever find another relationship. You may not trust yourself to choose a healthy partner. You may worry that no one else will want you. All these thoughts and feelings are normal and natural; they happen to everyone who leaves a relationship, abusive or not.

To grow through your worries and fears, you must first focus on yourself. Put thoughts of another relationship on the back burner. The right relationship will come at the right time, when you are ready. For now, it is more important to learn to be on your own, to cope in healthy ways with your loneliness and fears, to create a strong support system of people who truly love and respect you, and to be happy with yourself.

Practice loving yourself and being good to yourself. Your self-esteem needs rebuilding. Try to make time and to set aside a little money, if you can, to treat yourself to special outings or to purchase some personal goodies. You do not have to spend a lot of money. A few new things to wear, a new bedspread for your room, or some fresh flowers can make a big difference in your life. Even if you do not have any money to spend on yourself, you can treat yourself with things such as taking a long bath, making yourself hot chocolate, or taking a walk in the park. Make a list of all the things you can think of that make you feel good and do as many of these things as you can for yourself every day. In time, you will find your self-esteem and self-worth returning and you will begin to realize that your relationship with yourself is more important than any other relationship you can have.

BUILDING A RELATIONSHIP WITH SOMEONE ELSE

Hopefully, you have been taking care of yourself and working on your issues and problems in therapy or in a support group. Enough time has gone by—usually at least a year—and you have started thinking about the possibility of another relationship. How will you know what is a good relationship? How can you avoid falling into another abusive partnership? Here are some steps you can take to protect yourself.

1. Make a list of guidelines for a good relationship. Make another list of signs that warn of the danger of abuse. Post these lists where you can see them. Look at them often and think about them. When you meet someone, comparing his *actions* against the guidelines will help you to determine objectively if this person is someone you can consider becoming involved with.

2. When you first meet someone you are interested in, go slowly! The first three months of a relationship are the infatuation period. During infatuation you are not seeing the real person; you are only seeing who you want the person to be. Do not make any commitments during this period of time. If he pressures you to move quickly to a serious involvement or a commitment, realize that this is a danger sign and a red flag.

3. Watch his *actions*. Remember that words, promises, and explanations are easy, and they do not really tell you the truth about your partner. Put less value on what he says and more value on what he *does* and how he *behaves*. Notice if what he tells you about the past turns out to be true. Notice if he keeps his promises. *Notice his actions,* not his words.

4. Ask to meet other people who have been in his life—his family, his friends, his co-workers, his boss. Watch the way he interacts with these other people. See what their reactions are to him. Do they show love, affection, and acceptance toward him? Do they tell you nice things about him? Do they appear to be wanting to warn you to be careful? If he avoids taking you to spend time with his friends and family members, recognize this avoidance as a red flag; he is hiding something important from you that would not need to be hidden if he were an honest and open person seeking a real, meaningful relationship.

5. Take him to meet your family, friends, and co-workers. Ask them to tell you honestly what they think. *Take the opinions of your family and friends seriously.* Remember that they are not trying to keep you from being happy; they are only trying to protect you from your own unhealthy patterns. If they express concerns or disapprove of your relationship, this does not mean you must give the relationship up, but it is a yellow flag—a sign that you need to be very cautious about getting involved. You do not need to let your family or your friends choose your relationships for you, but your family and friends have been through other relationships with you and have seen the kinds of problems you have had in choosing a relationship.

Remember that your family and friends are not under the veil of illusion that your infatuation may be casting over your eyes. They may be able to see potential problems more realistically and more clearly than you can right now. Even if only a few of the significant people in your life express concerns and doubts about your love interest, take these concerns and doubts seriously. You may still want to continue exploring this relationship. If you do, take the concerns of your friends and family seriously and be cautious about your involvement. Be sure to pay particular attention to the behaviors that have caused those who love you to be concerned.

If your love interest avoids meeting with your friends and family or if he pouts and gripes about sharing you with them, recognize that this is red-flag behavior.

6. Wait at least one year before committing to live with or to marry a new partner. A year gives you the time you need to see him in a wide variety of situations. You need time to let infatuation fade and to begin to see the real person that you are interested in. You can see how he handles the variety of situations that happen in life. See what he does when something sad or stressful happens to him, and how he reacts when you are sad or stressed. See what happens when he gets angry at someone else and what happens when he gets angry at you. Try to face honestly how he reacts to situations and do not accept or make excuses for him. Measure his behavior against your list of guidelines. If he doesn't meet the guidelines, be willing to give up the relationship now, before you get in any deeper.

7. Pay close attention to your intuitive feelings and reactions. Your feelings are the key to your safety. If you feel "bad," "scared," "guilty," "worthless," "wrong," or "angry" in your relationship, it means you are not taking good care of yourself. You are concerning yourself more about his needs and feelings than about your own. This is the first step toward an unsafe relationship. If you experience negative feelings, your relationship needs careful evaluation. Although it is true that every relationship has problems, and that most couples have issues and disagreements, in a healthy relationship your problems, issues, and disagreements can be resolved without you feeling badly about yourself, and without you being physically hurt.

8. Contrary to what you may now believe, it is not true that every couple fights or that every relationship takes constant work. What is true is that every couple has differences and disagreements and that every relationship needs attention at times.

To help you make a good decision about a new relationship, be sure you see these signs of a healthy relationship:

1. He respects you as a separate and independent person. He treats you as an equal, not as less than himself nor as superior to himself. He respects your privacy and the other limits and boundaries you set for your own comfort and safety.
2. He is interested in hearing about your feelings, opinions, and interests. He wants to be a part of your life and he makes an effort to get to know your friends and family. He is open in sharing his own feelings, views, friends, family, and activities.
3. He asks your opinion in making decisions that will affect you. He considers your feelings and opinions to be legitimate and values them even when you disagree.
4. He is emotionally supportive when you are experiencing problems or stress in your life. You can count on him being caring and helpful when you are facing problems. He never uses your times of weakness or secrets you have shared with him to manipulate, punish, or take advantage of you.
5. He wants only a shared and equal sexual relationship. He is not interested in manipulating or forcing you to have sex when you don't feel comfortable.
6. He is not afraid of the normal differences between you and he is willing to negotiate and compromise to reach agreements that you are both comfortable with. He is more interested in resolving the problem so that you can be together than he is in winning the argument.
7. He encourages your personal, professional, and financial success. He is proud of, not threatened by, your accomplishments.
8. He manages his own negative feelings and reactions in an honest and mature way. When angry or upset, he can express himself without blaming, criticizing, or resorting to physical threats or physical violence.
9. He is financially responsible.
10. He is able to maintain his own separate identity while also being open to sharing himself and his life with a partner.

You may worry that you have been so hurt, so wounded, in your abusive relationship that you will not be able to recognize a good relationship or will not be able to let someone close to you again even if he is a good and loving person. Respect your worries and fears and use them to help remind you to be cautious about premature involvement. When you do start to become interested in someone, go slowly. If you have chosen a mature, responsible, loving person, he will understand why you are guarded and will be willing to work with you and give you the time you need to build up your trust in him. If he is impatient with you, criticizes you, or makes fun of your fears, he is not the person for you. After several months of being in a safe, secure relationship, you should notice that you are beginning to let down your guard and trust yourself and him. If after several months you still feel afraid and guarded, seek the guidance and help of a professional counselor. The counselor will help you differentiate between your own personal fears and things you may be seeing in the relationship that are a good cause for concern. If the relationship is safe but you are too afraid to let go and let yourself become intimate, therapy can help you to overcome your fears and risk loving again.

YOUR CHILDREN

While you are learning to take care of yourself, you may also have children to be concerned with. Your children may have many of the same feelings about and reactions to leaving the abusive home environment as you have. Most important to your children in making the adjustment to leaving is how you handle the situation. You can help the children make the change comfortably by behaving in a calm, confident way and by reassuring them that you are in control and that you will take care of everything.

Your children will go through a grief process. They may be as sad, angry, afraid, happy, relieved, and worried about the future as you are. They may, however, not have the same feelings at the same time as you do, and they may even have very different feelings from your own.

Your children will have had their own experience with your partner. They may or may not have been personally abused. The abuser may have manipulated their thoughts, beliefs, and feelings, just as he manipulated yours. Your children may be confused as well as frightened about your decision to leave.

Remember that your children may love your abuser and it may be hard for them to understand why you cannot stay with him. They may love him even if he also abused them. You must respect whatever feelings your children have and at the same time set healthy limits and boundaries for them. Tell them that it is okay to love their father (or whatever the relationship may be) but it is not okay that he has mistreated you or them. Be very firm when you tell them that it is never okay to be mean or to hurt or abuse someone, no matter how angry you are or what reason you think you have for your behavior. These are important messages for your children because they may have learned from watching your relationship that manipulation, control, and abuse are ways to get what you want. Tell your children that you, and they, deserve to be treated with love. You will not stay with someone who is abusive.

Your children may be angry at you for leaving and may blame you for all the problems that have happened in the family. Try not to take their anger personally. Often it is easier and safer for the children to be angry at the victim, the weaker person in the family, than at the abuser, who is someone they fear. If they do express anger and blame toward you, it means that you have made them feel safe enough for them to express themselves without fear of violence.

Try not to be defensive if your children express blame or anger toward you, but do set limits if your children try to verbally or physically abuse you. Tell your children that you respect their feelings and it is okay for them to talk to you about them, but you have made the best choices you can for all of you, and you expect them to respect your decisions even though they don't like them.

Children often have a hard time talking about their feelings or showing their emotions. They may act as if nothing has happened and may just go about their way being children, playing when they can and going off with their friends whenever they are allowed. Do not make the mistake of thinking that leaving is not bothering them. Instead, watch your children carefully for signs of distress and help them to express their feelings about the situation.

Here are some things you can do to help your children express their feelings:

1. If your children express some distress emotions either verbally or through their behavior, you can say, "I am noticing that you are (angry/sad/scared). I wonder if you are feeling this way because we have

left (Daddy). I feel some of these same feelings. Maybe we can talk about it."

2. If your children don't seem to want to talk, you can say, "I see that you are feeling (sad/scared/angry). . . . I want you to know it is okay for you to have your feelings and I am here if you would like to talk about them."

3. If your children don't want to talk to you about their feelings or about the situation, encourage them to write or draw about the situation. Provide your children with some toys that allow them to play out their feelings, such as dolls and a dollhouse, or a police car if the police were involved in stopping the violence. If your children are angry, a punching bag or a soft bat can be very helpful. Giving your children ways to express their feelings tells them you really mean it when you say that you respect how they feel.

4. If your children seem to want to talk but don't want to talk to you, ask them who they would be willing to talk to, and then help them make arrangements for some private time with this person. Let your children know that it is okay if they do not want to talk to you—you want to respect their privacy and their feelings—but that it is important that they talk to somebody so that their feelings do not build up and hurt them inside.

5. If your children are not talking about their anger or sadness but are withdrawing; regressing to babylike or clingy behavior; wetting or soiling themselves after they have been toilet trained; hitting other children; or their eating, sleeping, playing, or studying habits are upset, get professional help for them. A counselor can help your children find healthy ways to express their feelings and reactions. In the meantime, do not use this time to allow your children to become spoiled or out of control. Continue to set firm and consistent limits to prevent them from being destructive to themselves, to you, to others, or to animals or important possessions.

Remember that the most important thing your children need from you right now is to see that you can handle things, and to know that you love them and are concerned about the way the changes are affecting them. You can help your children by acting calmly and firmly in every situation, and by taking every opportunity to reassure them that your love for them will never go away.

Your children have been growing up in an unhealthy family and have seen or learned some unhealthy patterns of thinking and behaving. Just as you need to grow free, so do they. You are the key to their freedom to becoming healthy loving adults. You can grow free together.

NOTES

NOTES

NOTES

NOTES

Index

THE HAWORTH MALTREATMENT AND TRAUMA PRESS®
Robert A. Geffner, PhD
Senior Editor

IDENTIFYING CHILD MOLESTERS: PREVENTING CHILD SEXUAL ABUSE BY RECOGNIZING THE PATTERNS OF THE OFFENDERS by Carla van Dam. (2000). "The definitive work on the subject . . . . Provides parents and others with the tools to recognize when and how to intervene." *Roger W. Wolfe, MA, Co-Director, N. W. Treatment Associates, Seattle, Washington*

POLITICAL VIOLENCE AND THE PALESTINIAN FAMILY: IMPLICATIONS FOR MENTAL HEALTH AND WELL-BEING by Vivian Khamis. (2000). "A valuable book . . . a pioneering work that fills a glaring gap in the study of Palestinian society." *Elia Zureik, Professor of Sociology, Queens University, Kingston, Ontario, Canada*

STOPPING THE VIOLENCE: A GROUP MODEL TO CHANGE MEN'S ABUSIVE ATTITUDES AND BEHAVIORS by David J. Decker. (1999). "A concise and thorough manual to assist clinicians in learning the causes and dynamics of domestic violence." *Joanne Kittel, MSW, LICSW, Yachats, Oregon*

STOPPING THE VIOLENCE: A GROUP MODEL TO CHANGE MEN'S ABUSIVE ATTITUDES AND BEHAVIORS, THE CLIENT WORKBOOK by David J. Decker. (1999).

BREAKING THE SILENCE: GROUP THERAPY FOR CHILDHOOD SEXUAL ABUSE, A PRACTITIONER'S MANUAL by Judith A. Margolin. (1999). "This book is an extremely valuable and well-written resource for all therapists working with adult survivors of child sexual abuse." *Esther Deblinger, PhD, Associate Professor of Clinical Psychiatry, University of Medicine and Dentistry of New Jersey School of Osteopathic Medicine*

"I NEVER TOLD ANYONE THIS BEFORE": MANAGING THE INITIAL DISCLOSURE OF SEXUAL ABUSE RE-COLLECTIONS by Janice A. Gasker. (1999). "Discusses the elements needed to create a safe, therapeutic environment and offers the practitioner a number of useful strategies for responding appropriately to client disclosure." *Roberta G. Sands, PhD, Associate Professor, University of Pennsylvania School of Social Work*

FROM SURVIVING TO THRIVING: A THERAPIST'S GUIDE TO STAGE II RECOVERY FOR SURVIVORS OF CHILDHOOD ABUSE by Mary Bratton. (1999). "A must read for all, including survivors. Bratton takes a lifelong debilitating disorder and unravels its intricacies in concise, succinct, and understandable language." *Phillip A. Whitner, PhD, Sr. Staff Counselor, University Counseling Center, The University of Toledo, Ohio*

SIBLING ABUSE TRAUMA: ASSESSMENT AND INTERVENTION STRATEGIES FOR CHILDREN, FAMILIES, AND ADULTS by John V. Caffaro and Allison Conn-Caffaro. (1998). "One area that has almost consistently been ignored in the research and writing on child maltreatment is the area of sibling abuse. This book is a welcome and required addition to the developing literature on abuse." *Judith L. Alpert, PhD, Professor of Applied Psychology, New York University*

BEARING WITNESS: VIOLENCE AND COLLECTIVE RESPONSIBILITY by Sandra L. Bloom and Michael Reichert. (1998). "A totally convincing argument. . . . Demands careful study by all elected representatives, the clergy, the mental health and medical professions, representatives of the media, and all those unwittingly involved in this repressive perpetuation and catastrophic global problem." *Harold I. Eist, MD, Past President, American Psychiatric Association*

TREATING CHILDREN WITH SEXUALLY ABUSIVE BEHAVIOR PROBLEMS: GUIDELINES FOR CHILD AND PARENT INTERVENTION by Jan Ellen Burton, Lucinda A. Rasmussen, Julie Bradshaw, Barbara J. Christopherson, and Steven C. Huke. (1998). "An extremely readable book that is well-documented and a mine of valuable 'hands on' information. . . . This is a book that all those who work with sexually abusive children or want to work with them must read." *Sharon K. Araji, PhD, Professor of Sociology, University of Alaska, Anchorage*

THE LEARNING ABOUT MYSELF (LAMS) PROGRAM FOR AT-RISK PARENTS: LEARNING FROM THE PAST—CHANGING THE FUTURE by Verna Rickard. (1998). "This program should be a part of the resource materials of every mental health professional trusted with the responsibility of working with 'at-risk' parents." *Terry King, PhD, Clinical Psychologist, Federal Bureau of Prisons, Catlettsburg, Kentucky*

THE LEARNING ABOUT MYSELF (LAMS) PROGRAM FOR AT-RISK PARENTS: HANDBOOK FOR GROUP PARTICIPANTS by Verna Rickard. (1998). "Not only is the LAMS program designed to be educational and build skills for future use, it is also fun!" *Martha Morrison Dore, PhD, Associate Professor of Social Work, Columbia University, New York, New York*

BRIDGING WORLDS: UNDERSTANDING AND FACILITATING ADOLESCENT RECOVERY FROM THE TRAUMA OF ABUSE by Joycee Kennedy and Carol McCarthy. (1998). "An extraordinary survey of the history of child neglect and abuse in America. . . . A wonderful teaching tool at the university level, but should be required reading in high schools as well." *Florabel Kinsler, PhD, BCD, LCSW, Licensed Clinical Social Worker, Los Angeles, California*

CEDAR HOUSE: A MODEL CHILD ABUSE TREATMENT PROGRAM by Bobbi Kendig with Clara Lowry. (1998). "Kendig and Lowry truly . . . realize the saying that we are our brothers' keepers. Their spirit permeates this volume, and that spirit of caring is what always makes the difference for people in painful situations." *Hershel K. Swinger, PhD, Clinical Director, Children's Institute International, Los Angeles, California*

SEXUAL, PHYSICAL, AND EMOTIONAL ABUSE IN OUT-OF-HOME CARE: PREVENTION SKILLS FOR AT-RISK CHILDREN by Toni Cavanagh Johnson and Associates. (1997). "Professionals who make dispositional decisions or who are related to out-of-home care for children could benefit from reading and following the curriculum of this book with children in placements." *Issues in Child Abuse Accusations*

Order Your Own Copy of
This Important Book for Your Personal Library!

GROWING FREE
A Manual for Survivors of Domestic Violence

_____in softbound at $14.95 (ISBN: 0-7890-1280-4)

COST OF BOOKS_____

OUTSIDE USA/CANADA/
MEXICO: ADD 20%_____

POSTAGE & HANDLING_____
(US: $4.00 for first book & $1.50
for each additional book)
Outside US: $5.00 for first book
& $2.00 for each additional book)

SUBTOTAL_____

in Canada: add 7% GST_____

STATE TAX_____
(NY, OH & MIN residents, please
add appropriate local sales tax)

FINAL TOTAL_____
(If paying in Canadian funds,
convert using the current
exchange rate, UNESCO
coupons welcome.)

Prices in US dollars and subject to change without notice.

❏   **BILL ME LATER:** ($5 service charge will be added)
(Bill-me option is good on US/Canada/Mexico orders only;
not good to jobbers, wholesalers, or subscription agencies.)

❏ Check here if billing address is different from
shipping address and attach purchase order and
billing address information.

Signature_____

❏   **PAYMENT ENCLOSED: $**_____

❏   **PLEASE CHARGE TO MY CREDIT CARD.**

❏ Visa   ❏ MasterCard   ❏ AmEx   ❏ Discover
❏ Diner's Club   ❏ Eurocard   ❏ JCB

Account # _____

Exp. Date_____

Signature_____

NAME_____

INSTITUTION_____

ADDRESS_____

CITY_____

STATE/ZIP_____

COUNTRY_____ COUNTY (NY residents only)_____

TEL_____ FAX_____

E-MAIL_____

May we use your e-mail address for confirmations and other types of information? ❏ Yes   ❏ No
We appreciate receiving your e-mail address and fax number. Haworth would like to e-mail or fax special
discount offers to you, as a preferred customer. **We will never share, rent, or exchange your e-mail address
or fax number.** We regard such actions as an invasion of your privacy.

Order From Your Local Bookstore or Directly From
The Haworth Press, Inc.
10 Alice Street, Binghamton, New York 13904-1580 • USA
TELEPHONE: 1-800-HAWORTH (1-800-429-6784) / Outside US/Canada: (607) 722-5857
FAX: 1-800-895-0582 / Outside US/Canada: (607) 722-6362
E-mail: getinfo@haworthpressinc.com
PLEASE PHOTOCOPY THIS FORM FOR YOUR PERSONAL USE.
www.HaworthPress.com

BOF00

ML   6/02